"Cross Between the

The Sporting Recollections
of
Fr. Francis Fleming S.J. during The Great War.

Edited by Robert Wilkinson.

Illustrated by Bertie de Lisle.

Dedicated to the memory of all country sportsmen
who went to war.

Prayer of the Huntsman.

Great St. Hubert, bless all who gather here in this natural setting, whose aim is to follow in your footsteps to be skilled and ethical hunters. Grant us confidence, perseverance, patience and the accuracy to increase our proficiency in the fields and forests.

Published 2021 by The Beaumont Union & Glassingall Books

glassingall@aol.com

ISBN: 978-1-9164295-8-1

A catalogue record for this book is available from The British
Library

This Book is sold in aid of HOUNDS FOR HEROES.
The Charity provides specially trained assistance dogs to injured and
disabled men and women of both the UK Armed Forces and
Emergency Services.

houndsforheroes.com

Printed and bound by Witley Press, Hunstanton,
Norfolk, PE36 6AD

CONTENTS

PREFACE

The Right Reverend Richard Moth Bishop of Arundel and Brighton, previously Bishop of the Forces.

The view from a horse provides a different perspective on the world, as does that gained from the fisherman's reflective place on the riverbank. The consolation provided by a faithful hound is well documented. Such perspectives are brought to the reader of this Memoir, written in the often-dreadful circumstances of the First World War and provides a lively account of the experience of a chaplain who also brought solace, prayer and moments of peace to the soldiers he served.

This work is a welcome addition to the large body of works about that Conflict, enlivened by fine illustrations. It serves, too, as a reminder of the continuing ministry of Chaplains, whose presence is so important to all who serve in the Armed Forces of the world.

+Richard

Rt. Rev. Richard Moth.

"The Sporting Chaplain."

INTRODUCTION

"To Fr. Francis."

The setting of these recollections is The Great War but there is little of its conduct, save for a reflection on certain individuals. The writer is an army Chaplain but there is scant coverage of his ministry. What we have is a story of country sport enjoyed in the most unlikely setting, behind the front line, by a man who was a poacher's collaborator, a whipper-in to a motley pack of hounds and certainly a contented fisherman. Will Ogilvie wrote in his poem *"The True Sportsman."*

All the best and truest sportsmen I have lived with
And have known
Have a changeless faith within them which their
Simple hearts enthrone,
Believing in the God that made the green fields
Passing fair,
The God that gave good courage – and to every man
His share.

Reading these short memoirs, I felt that this verse could be the epitaph for the author of these stories. Stories that differ from the more usual tales of life at the Front.

I came across them in copies of a school journal – *The Beaumont Review*: a periodical, which at the time, just after the First World War, was as much written for the school's Old Boys as it was for that generation of pupils. The author wrote under the pseudonym of "Khaki Palmer" and this happened to be one Fr. Francis Fleming SJ. The articles were drawn from the diaries that he kept at the time of his military service.

As a priest fond of country sports, Fr Francis would have been well aware of the legend of St. Hubert. Back in the mid-600s, a young Frenchman, Duke Hubert of Aquitaine was out enjoying the countryside on Good Friday. He was on his steed taking part in his favourite pastime: hunting. The problem was that he was supposed to be in church that day. However, hunting stag seemed more important to him at the time, so a-stag-hunting he went.

Hubert did find the "hart" he was looking for, only this particular stag was different from those found in the past. When he trotted his horse over to investigate the animal that was held to bay by his hounds, he found that there was a glowing crucifix above its head. At the same time, he heard a voice admonishing him to repent of his misspent life. And so, Hubert swiftly asked forgiveness. He climbed off his horse and begged penance for his sins. He later became a priest, and finally Bishop of Liege. Throughout his ministry, St. Hubert maintained his passion for hunting. He integrated the chase into his ministry, and he even kept his hounds and enjoyed the sport in his clerical life. He was popular with the local huntsmen, and spread Christianity throughout the Ardennes Forest region. Some have said that the deer lectured Hubert on how to hunt — that he should only go after the older stags who were past their breeding age, that men should respect animals, and that the huntsman should attack only when a quick kill was assured.

This legend lent itself to the title of this short memoir "Cross between the Antlers": apt indeed, as you will read, for Fr. Francis Fleming.

So, what of the man? He came from a well-to-do Anglo-Irish family. His grandfather James, a barrister and QC, spent five years with a claim before the House of Lords for an ancient Irish Baronetcy, Baron Slane, which eventually failed on insufficient evidence. His father was also a barrister, and both an uncle and a great uncle were

"Beaumont."

knighted for colonial service. Francis was born at Templeogue near
Dublin in 1876, a village between the Rivers Poodle and Dodder and
it is evident from the empathy of his writing that he had a great love
of the Irish people and the countryside, this despite spending much
of his youth at school in England or at the family's London address
in Charles Street off Berkeley Square.

Francis was sent to Beaumont, a small Catholic school at Old
Windsor run by the Jesuits and of increasing prestige. Queen Victoria
had already visited on a couple of occasions and the Rector at the

time was Sir William Heathcote Bt., known affectionately by the boys as "The Gen" for his military bearing and command of those in his care, and the obedience of his two red setters that followed him everywhere.

The countryside there, at that epoch, was said to be idyllic and the poet Peter Levi captured this when he wrote:

"The essential character of Beaumont, whose buildings are one of the minor excitements of a relaxed and unpretentious landscape, exists in a perpetual tendency of the school, the estate and the village to subdue themselves to the river. The lower Thames, too tame to dominate even its tame surroundings, moves through them like an ageing and purposeless divinity, shabbily, creating as it goes: all those river-meadows with their ragged elm hedges, the mists and buttercups and sinuous variations". John Denham understood the picturesque qualities of this countryside in his poem Cooper's Hill, as did brooding Shelley who walked nearby as his meditations of 'Alastor' took shape. At the same period, Paul Sandby drew and painted: his restraint of colour, and his dry and sober light, preserve, with perfect realism, a world of masses and forms and relations which is exactly the country in which Beaumont was situated".

The young Fleming was fortunate to find himself in these relaxing grounds with the opportunity to ride, as the College kept horses, follow hounds and enjoy the flora and fauna.

"Beaumont kept horses."

Francis was remembered as being diffident of his capabilities, but was none the less a good sportsman and played in probably the best Soccer XI the school produced winning all its matches by very large scores. Though not in the Cricket XI, he had a reputation for a smasher of bats "sending the remnants in the direction of mid-off". Francis had a fair number of kindred sporting spirits in his year at school and from a similar Irish background: Charles Lynch would become Master of the South Union hounds, Arthur McCann, Leonard Morrogh-Ryan and Vere Brudenell-Murphy hunted, raced and all played polo for Ireland. However, Francis decided on a different course and on leaving the school in 1894, he entered the Jesuit Order in England to train for the priesthood. Many of the years of study and ordination were spent at Stonyhurst, the Jesuits' renowned college in the "wilds" of Lancashire. Here he would have enjoyed the fishing on the Hodder which rises in the Forest of Bowland, then runs through the estate on its way to join The Ribble.

The Jesuits, rather similar to the army, like to "change your posting" from time to time so, following ordination, Francis was sent back to Beaumont in 1911 as a member of the staff to teach one of the junior classes. With him was another of his old school contemporaries and friend - Francis Devas.

At the outbreak of War in 1914, both of them volunteered to become chaplains but the Provincial of the Society could only spare a dozen from his limited resources at the time; later that number would grow to over eighty. Francis Devas and their one-time Headmaster "The Gen" William Heathcote were both accepted – Francis Fleming would have to wait. Francis was not from a military background but his younger brother Baldwyn, two years his junior at school, had gained a commission in The Duke of Cambridge's Own (Middlesex Regiment) and had served in South Africa against the Boers at both Spion Kop and Alleman's Nek. He was now a company commander preparing to deploy to France. Understandably, Francis wanted to go as well but he was made to wait two years before getting his wish. Most of those who volunteered as a Padre were new to such challenges – Francis had no experience of working with soldiers and certainly not of warfare, though Beaumont was probably no different from many schools that were going through a period of patriotic fervour, with emphasis on the military with the formation of The Officer Training Corps following the War in South Africa.

As all men of the cloth, Francis wanted to do his best and support those under his pastoral care. Chaplains needed to be physically fit with an ability to ride a horse and ideally speak foreign languages, but they embarked on overseas service with no special training and very little guidance about the nature of the task ahead of them. In many instances, they had to carve out a role for themselves in a hostile environment the clergy in the home country would find difficult to comprehend. Many chaplains left diaries and letters, the majority of which have never been published. Those that were provide a unique insight into life with the troops, seen through the eyes of men who owed their first allegiance to their Church rather than to the Army whose uniform they wore. Not only did they provide spiritual guidance and sustenance to the soldiers and being with them at their hour of need, they were major contributors to general morale, being part of the team and enjoying many of the hobbies and sport of their "flock". Usually this would include such games as soccer, rugby or cricket, playing cards and "sing songs". I think it is fair to say that the activities of Fr Francis and his friends were a little unorthodox and not what one would normally expect as part of life during the war.

"Khaki Palmer" takes up his story from the land where St. Hubert enjoyed his sport.

"The France that awaited him."

CHAPTER ONE
"Concerning certain lapses."

Moralists tell us that circumstances may excuse us from the observance of merely human laws: and the Laws of Sport are, in the main, merely human laws. Therefore, this is not a dissertation on the ethics of sportsmanship; but the writer is a typical OB (Old Beaumont Boy) in that he has an innate but very well concealed respect for every form of law: He would no more think of poaching his neighbour's preserved stickle-back or sparrow than he would of burgling the Crown Jewels; and, before placing these impenitent confessions before the law-loving readers of *The Beaumont Review*, he wishes to plead circumstances as a justification for doings, which in the normal course of events he would have been the first to condemn.

Further, he would mention that, although the Censor has been relegated to other spheres of usefulness, those stout fellows who, during the War, put in such sterling work from the Godbert (1) even to the meaner hostels about Fleet Street, are now free to print whatsoever their fancy prompts. There are even more awesome things in this world than a trial under the provisions of D.O.R.A. (Defence of the Realm Act), in consideration of which the names of the players and places which appear on this veracious page are discreetly camouflaged!

"The Royal Field Artillery (RFA)."

It was in the Autumn of 1916 that the writer was first introduced to the War, at which time the distinguished R.F.A. Brigade, to whose kindly care he was committed, had its waggon lines on the outskirts of a hamlet, which shall be called Saint Gervais, some five or six miles behind the Front line.

The surrounding country was made up of wide, unfenced fields already two seasons fallow, with stretches of snug covert set between. On the second day after his arrival he discovered the existence of a fair number of pheasants - and of MacMorrough !

In the course of a stroll, he was watching a couple of the former scratching for their evening meal, when he became aware that someone else was similarly interested. A tall spare figure, hardly distinguishable from the background of October leaves, was moving noiselessly through the bushes towards the happy unsuspecting diners.

When he was within some twenty yards of them, he took something from the breast of his tunic, tossed it on the ground, and stepped back among the hazels. At once that something stretched, shook itself, and crowed. The cock pheasant answered the challenge, and without further delay they joined. For about half a minute there was a whirling tumble of bright-hued feathers, then something seemed to collapse, and a lean steel-spurred gamecock (2), rearing himself up over his fallen foe, proclaimed his victory to the world.

From his hiding-place came the greeny-brown shadow; the gamecock went back inside the tunic without protest, and its late opponent disappeared, so far as could be seen, inside the loose cut gunner's breeches.

Save for a fluttering feather or two and a few beads of blood, the whole tragedy had been absorbed in the person of its maker, and he was threading his way catlike away among the trees. Here was a Corporal – the stripes on his sleeve shewed dimly – out of bounds, improperly dressed, and, in defiance of half-a-dozen severally

"A whirling Tumble of bright-hued feathers."

stringent G.R.O.'s, (General Routine Orders) engaged in the pursuit of game, the property of our Allies. By virtue of the brand-new stars upon his shoulder straps, the writer was well aware that he must know nothing of all these things; but this form of poaching was irresistibly fascinating, and he started with small stealth that was in him, to hunt the hunter.

Little more than a hundred yards on, there was a clearing among the trees. Again, the cock was tossed upon the grass; there was the preliminary flapping of wings to right the ruffled plumage; the shrill defiance, answered from the under-growth; the stately entrance of a cock pheasant to see who thus invaded his domain. Again the two perfect strangers hurled themselves at one another, and once more, after an even briefer battle than before, the cock reposed upon his owner's bosom, and the pheasant rested elsewhere upon his person.

Then, as the scribe moved to follow towards the scene of the next act, a stick snapped under his foot. Straightway, he was intent on lighting a cigarette; but either because the acting was not good enough, or for some reason of his own, the Corporal decided not to avail himself of the proffered loophole for escape, but stood gazing

"Good Evenin', your Reverence Father."

into the tangle of brambles before him. When the cigarette was alight, he clicked to attention and saluted, smart as a guardsman, despite the bulging unbuttoned tunic; and, as he cut his hand away, murmured in a voice, whose music could only come from west of The Shannon, "Good evenin', your Reverence Father".

Note (1): Godbert refers to the "Restaurant Godbert" at Amiens, popular with important personalities, senior officers and journalists.

Note (2): Using a spurred cock for hunting was not unknown at the time and cockfighting is still legal under the penal code in certain villages of North East France where there has been an uninterrupted tradition.

"Sucked their doodeens."

CHAPTER TWO

"Introducing the poacher."

Thus, it was that MacMorrough and the writer became acquainted. MacMorrough, despite occasional failings, was a leading light in the writer's flock, and furthermore was soon his most valued friend.

Perhaps one day, when the Editor of *The Review* lacks better copy, he may print some extracts from the chronicle of MacMorrough as the scribe knew him, and as he himself told the tale in the Chaplain's tent, or as they jogged up together to the gun pits before the rumbling limbers, met in the horse lines, or sucked their "doodeens" (3) in the shelter of some wood.

The day after that first meeting, a brace of cock pheasants appeared in the officers' mess-house sent in for the Padre by Corporal MacMorrough, who had "picked them up." Later, he explained that Routine Orders forbade the killing of game but said nothing about the gathering of such as was already dead. He thought these pheasants might get killed in the fighting; some of them were indeed gashed, as though they had hurt themselves on the wire, which in the War was woven web-like over the face of this land. Sad to relate, as intimacy grew, it became clear that the Corporal did not limit himself to the collecting of game whose tale of days was already done.

One morning he was surprised twisting sundry familiar sheets of slate-grey paper into cones, like those in which grocers of old used to dispense their smaller merchandise. Each was fastened at the side with a pin and smeared within with a mixture of surprising stickiness. At first, he was not inclined to be communicative, and muttered something about things that "officers did not ought to be knowing about", but later, after some remarks as to a priest's ability to keep a secret, mentioned that he would be along the lower side of a certain covert after tea.

The appointed hour and place found him equipped with a score of his paper bags, a heel-peg and a pocket-full of raisins scrounged from the cooks. The proceedings consisted of making a series of holes with the peg, as a gardener 'dibbles' holes for the reception of young plants. In each hole was loosely fitted one of the limed cones, and into this was dropped a raisin, fragments of the fruit being scattered up to the covert edge. This and other carefully chosen spots, it seemed, had been sown daily with a few chopped up raisins for a week or more.

When all was ready, he withdrew behind a clump of tall weeds, and squatted down to watch. Slowly the minutes crawled by.

The shadows dragged across the grass, while little breezes whispered among the branches, and the layered clouds to westward turned from snow to ivory, and from ivory to flaming gold.

At length there was a scratching of dead leaves in the copse-wood, which ceased, and began, and ceased again three or four times; and at last a hen pheasant stepped daintily into the open. Presently, she found something that pleased her among the grass, and gave a little cluck of satisfaction, then another, and another; and a demure brown sister joined her in her search. After some minutes, she came to one of the raisin-bated holes, looked into it, hesitated, and finally made a dive at the fatal fruit, only to withdraw her head fast bonneted with a grey extinguisher. She did not seem alarmed in the beginning and tried to scratch away the blinding encumbrance from her eyes; but her efforts only fixed it more tightly. Her nerve failed, and she began to run this way and that; and then soft-footed fate in the person of MacMorrough overtook her: a cut with an ash plant across her outstretched neck, and she went to her rest in the adapted sandbag which he wore inside the skirts of his jacket, while he returned to watch behind his breastwork of weeds.

Again, a long wait, while a foraging mole threw up his covered trench across the turf, a pair of field-mice cheeped and chivvied close at hand, and a nightingale filled heaven and earth with song.

Then once more, Eve learnt the fateful lesson of the forbidden fruit, and took her place with her sister in the sandbag. By the time the sky had lost its lingering crimson and the last of his victims' fellows had gone to their roost, MacMorrough's spare person was a Falstaffian deformity with three hens and a cock concealed about it.

"They might get killed in the fighting."

One of the most striking things in the forward areas were the partridges one saw there. Miles of open country, in peace-time cultivated to the last inch, had been lying neglected for a couple of years, and were covered with a growth of grasses, weeds, and self-sown grain, that made ideal partridge cover, and afforded unlimited food. The appalling noises of modern warfare troubled the little brown bird not a whit, and it was a common thing to see a covey feeding or dusting themselves within a stone's throw of a battery of crashing eighteen-pounders, or taking short untroubled flights among the hidden pits, whence the big howitzers launched their roaring messengers.

It was said that a plane droning overhead made them lie close; but this they always did and it is certain that the Armistice found the birds thick in regions, over which aircraft had flown and fought for four years; nor was it unusual to find them quite near to where the machines were taking off and landing at all hours of the day and night. In his pursuit of the pheasant, MacMorrough's methods displayed originality "rather than finesse". Given the pair of perfectly trained cocks, which jolted with him from place to place in their padded ammunition box on the spare harness waggon, or the knowledge of the bird-limed cones, any reasonably intelligent person might seemingly have added a pheasant to his rations, if he happened to be in their neighbourhood.

In the taking of partridges, however, the Corporal shewed real skill and a deep acquaintance with his quarry's ways. His favourite method was a snare of twisted horsehair, set with a bent stick and a sort of trigger arrangement, which released the spring when a bird touched it. The whole contrivance called for great niceness in its making, and for knowledge in the choice of a site and the effective placing of its parts. Considerable numbers of these traps were set in likely spots and were visited in the course of the morning and at dusk. The best day's bag the writer knows of was eight brace. He spoke, also, of taking partridges with limed twigs and leaves, but this "had the birds in the divil's mess, and ruinated your kit" when you bestowed them about your person. Also, he had a scheme of making a long net out of camouflage sheets from which the rags and raffia had been removed, but the thick ground cover would have been a great obstacle to its use; besides which absence from camp at night except on duty, and any form of unauthorised activity during the hours of darkness, would have meant trouble for a certainty.

"Hares were few in those parts."

Hares were few in those parts, but four or five of the steel strands from a field telephone wire, heated to remove their temper and twisted together, made an excellent noose. And it may be mentioned that "pussy" (4), who put her head into a snare of MacMorrough's setting, broke her neck incontinently, and lay quiet until collected; unlike her sister in the wire of a less skilled practitioner, whose shrieks and struggles advertised the neighbourhood of her fate, and possibly meant a lurking M.P. when the trapper came that way.

And so the days sped by. Days that introduced the scribe to many things besides unorthodox pot-hunting. Mass said and the Sacraments administered in undreamt-of settings; mud *in excelsis*, and cold, and filth, and manifold discomforts, hardly noticed because a cheery world took them all as part of the game; invisible things that came rumbling or screaming out of the distance and finished their song in cataclysmic crashes; pain and mangled limbs and blanket-wrapped relics dumbly appealing beside the shallow trench for the last loving that Mother Church gives to her children.

Note (3): Doodeen or Dudeen – a short-stemmed Irish pipe.
Note (4); The Hare's nickname comes from the latin - Lepus.
A shared one with rabbits but more notably with cats.

"Farewell to the Gunners."

CHAPTER THREE

"Chasse à pied."

Then the unseen powers that shuffled the pieces on the board bethought them of this pawn, and a pink signals form came up from Divisional H.Q. directing him to proceed forthwith to a highly specialized corps, whose name might not be spoken, nor its lurking place revealed, and which could only be approached by roundabout stages, each section of the journey a plunge into the unknown, to be continued in accordance with orders which should be waiting at its end.

This mysterious destination was reached at last, and there the writer found the bravest and best of good fellows, and sport in plenty, both approved by custom and entirely new. It was in the early days of 1917, when it was the writer's privilege to be attached to the Heavy Branch of the Machine Gun Corps. That body, after a small beginning on the Somme in the previous year, had been expanded to four battalions, which, with Headquarters and workshops, were in winter quarters, hidden away among half-a-dozen villages in a quiet valley some thirty miles behind the Front. That small beginning, giving away as it did the priceless factor of surprise, had been made against the better judgment of all connected with the Corps; but it had been rendered

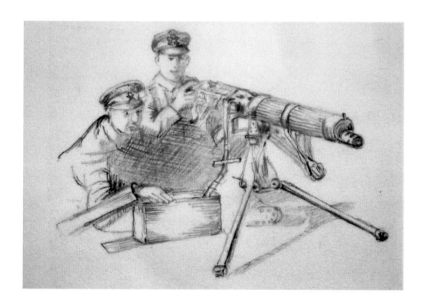

"Gun drills."

necessary by the attitude of the Great Ones, who flatly refused to consider preparations on a large scale, until the new arm should have proved its value on a small one.

Life was a feverish business in those days. The building of newly joined officers and men into sections, companies, and battalions; schemings and contrivings to make good the want of every sort of equipment; instructions, drills, and practices with six-pounder Lewis gun, bomb, revolver, and a score of technical gadgets; tactical exercises; compass marches; lectures; inspections; cross-country runs; rugger matches; snow fights; the provision and betterment of billets, cook houses, canteens, and other accommodation; sanitation; stores and the supplying of a thousand other needs, But whatever the new force lacked, its human material, from the Brigadier to the cook's mates, was of the finest.

Anything below first-class found it advisable to apply for a re-transfer to the unit from which it came, so every day saw crews and sections welded into more perfect wholes; growing pride and rivalry between individuals and companies; increasing knowledge and confidence between officers and men; and the development of A. and O. organisation (5), the nervous system on which the life of the whole body depends. Looked back upon, it was perhaps the most wonderful thing the writer came into personal contact with during the War – this evolution of a novel, highly skilled, and wholly efficient fighting machine, where a couple of months previously there had been, save among a few experts, complete technical ignorance, and chaos almost as complete.

18

Still, mighty as the work was, there were corners in the soul of certain British officers it could not fill, even when supplemented by rather pokerish bridge and the allurements of the gramophone. Instinctively if inarticulately the majority of these souls cried out for sport. Toby was our Master of Hounds, and around him our varied sporting essays chiefly centred. July 1914 had seen him busy with puppies and porridge, and poultry funds. Then the unthinkable had happened, and a few weeks later he was leading his squadron in sterner chases than he had ever ridden in the Shires to music far different from that of his dappled darlings.

He had played his part in the wonderful work our Cavalry did during the nightmare days of the Retreat, and gathered his DSO, on the hills above Bailleul (6).

When the war settled down to an affair of trenches, the horse soldiers' occupation was for the time being gone; and, when discreet but promising whispers came his way concerning a mysterious development of the "Emma Gees" (7). Toby had volunteered for the new adventure in the fruitful expectation of fun. From his kennels, there had followed him to the War a couple of useful hunters and a brace of most workmanlike terriers; and these same four comrades, by some masterpiece of wangling, accompanied him in his migration to the M.G.C. Besides Teddy and Viper, the aforesaid terriers, there owed him a somewhat independent allegiance Donner and Blitzen, greyhounds and stout Britons (in all but figure) in spite of their name. There was Nipper, in pedigree the offspring of whippet and sheep-dog, and in appearance a Borzoi gone badly wrong, and Tinker, a most lovable, but sadly imbecilic, black mongrel. And with this pack we hunted many things, including even the royal red varmint himself; and that in such manner as it is doubtful if he had ever been hunted before.

With Toby as huntsman and the scribe as whipper-in, rats were our first quarries, and they gave unfailing entertainment whenever we were not bent on higher game. In point, both of numbers and of size, the rats of the particular village were of the aristocracy of ratdom. Every house of any pretensions had its ancestral manure heap before its front door, and these were the scenes of our first efforts. To begin with, the natives were inclined to resent our assaults on their treasured accumulations; but when they realized (the idea seemed to have escaped them heretofore) that the mischievous rodent had his dwelling therein, toothless patriarchs and grubby youngsters, encouraged by their shrieking women folk, armed themselves with pitchforks and cudgels and joined in the fray. To see those past and future soldiers of France hurl themselves at the festering mess, and to hear their yells when *Mus Norvegicus* broke cover- *"A bas le Rat"*, *"Vilain Boche"*, *"Sale Polisson"*, etc., etc., was to understand something of the qualities which make a French battalion with the bayonet one of the most terrible things in the world. Unfortunately, they got badly bitten with the game, and the *"chasse au fumier"* became so popular that those promising coverts were soon worked out.

Consequently, we turned our attention to outlying farm steadings and honeycombed banks, where friend Rat was always at home; but to penetrate these fastnesses was quite another thing. The pack, except the long dogs, did their best; but the enemy had things pretty well his own way. Next a pair of ferrets was produced from somewhere, and they did good work; but the odds against them were too heavy, and they got so badly punished that they refused to work anymore.

"A hunting we will go."

Then the scribe bethought him of a method invented by a certain fertile poacher not unknown in the editorial offices of *The Beaumont Review.*

Carbide is introduced at the lowest point of a system of rat-holes, water poured upon it, and the hole closed with a sod. The resulting acetylene finds its way along the runs, and the dwellers therein, faced with the choice between being gassed and bolting, generally prefer the latter. If things get slow, a light is applied to the mouth of a hole, and, when the gas has had time to penetrate the labyrinth, produces quite surprising results.

One of our Majors, who had come back to do his bit from the wild places behind Zanzibar, and who could assume an entirely respectable semblance of boredom in the presence of "five nines" (8), was smitten with something very like shell shock, when the mud-walled sty in which he was operating resolved itself into its component dust, and the floor arose and struck him in the teeth, while lambent flames removed most of his moustache and eyebrows. Petrol, poured down the holes well to wind-ward, and lighted, worked fairly well, but was less certain and less vigorous than the acetylene. Later, when smoke-bombs first made their appearance, these were employed with good effect. But the best thing we came across was that used by the Heavy Gunners, who light a bundle of tubular big-gun cordite in their victims' dwellings; the nitrous fumes from this would bolt a bum-bailiff.

"A great red fox."

The exploration of rat holes led in natural sequence to rabbit burrows; but our Mess President was pushing a line of tinned Australian rabbit just then, and somehow bunny failed to intrigue us. But one day, when Teddy and Viper had dug themselves in and their muffled yaps

were betraying a quite unusual degree of excitement, from the far end
of the burrow there slunk away through the bushes a great red fox.
Toby hulloo'd him, and we tried to get Nipper on to his line, but that
worthy was so frantic that he could not hold it for a yard, while the
greyhounds, hunting as they do by sight, were quite useless. We had
all rushed to the top of the bank, when the vixen dashed out below
us, and made for another covert half-a-mile away across the stubble.
This time Donner and Blitzen viewed her, and the whole hunt were
away for what their respective legs were worth. She was three-
quarters of the way towards safety when Blitzen snapped her. She
turned, however and snapped back, and was promptly dropped.
Then Donner rolled her over and was bitten through the foreleg for
his pains. But by that time Nipper had come up, whose ring-craft was
more brutally business-like than that of his aristocratic colleagues, and
he had her by the throat in a twinkling. Soon the terriers arrived, and
that was our first kill.

24

The Pack, though they worried her delightedly, absolutely refused to break up the carcase, which was left on the field; and some local economist skinned it and realized twenty francs for the pelt-minus the brush, which Toby had whipped off with the aid of one of his boot laces. After that we were on the look-out for earths and had much hunting; but as a rule, these abodes were well inside coverts thickly dotted with refuges, and only once or twice afterwards did we get a run in the open. Most of our foxes were chopped as they bolted, and two or three were killed by the terriers underground.

In the course of our search for fox-earths we discovered the presence of badgers. And these Teddy and Viper went for gamely enough, but Brother Brock could never be persuaded to tempt fortune in the open. We poured out much honest sweat, and removed many tons of earth, but he invariably chose spots where the limestone out-cropped and usually under the roots of forest trees, so that we never got to close quarters with the gentleman.

Père Mich – he was not an ecclesiastic, but a decayed retainer from the neighbouring chateau – volunteered to show us how to bring him into the daylight; but his sporting outfit consisted of a couple of large salmon gaffs and a sort of grapnel at the end of a flexible steel rod, so we thought we liked our own futile methods best. Neither did gas seem a fit weapon against a foeman of such worth.

Our most orthodox form of sport, and probably our best, was coursing. True, in the innermost depths of our consciences there was an unvoiced misgiving that G.H.Q. had sometime permitted itself expressions which I might be held to discourage, but we had the broad valley to ourselves and, save on a couple of main roads, Brass Hats, A.P.M.'s (9), and such, were unknown there.

Indeed, there were miles of gently rolling country, unfenced, and at that time under stubble, plough, and winter wheat – the last too backward to be damaged – with occasional patches of pasture and lucerne if we did happen to stray across it.

"Strong, but very wild."

Unlike around St Gervais, hares were plentiful and strong, but very wild, and cover was scanty; so that they generally got away with a long start. Donner and Blitzen, though of far above average quality, were time and again dead beat; while we, not-withstanding Puss's kindly habit of ringing, were often near rupturing lung and muscle in our struggles to keep the chase in view as it passed over the ever-recurring rises. Nevertheless, a very fair number of hares did find their way inside the linings of our tunics, to the no small improvement of soup and stew.

While the snow was on the ground, one two of us, with white nightshirts over our clothes, tried stalking partridges with field glasses and a little .22 rifle. This met with a fair measure of success when there was wind enough to drown the noise of our crawling. At other times we could never get near them. Meanwhile the forging of our weapon went on apace, and when the first touches of green began to show in wood and hedgerow, the word came that sent us forth once more to that bigger field, where the chances were not all on our side. (The Battle of Cambrai in November).

Note (5): Administration and Ordnance Organisation.

Note (6): The identity of Toby is unknown but it would seem he was a Yeomanry Officer and an MFH at home.

Note (7): The "Emma Gees" nickname given to The Machine Gun Corps soon to be known as The Tank Corps.

Note (8): The author probably uses the term "five-nines" because it seems more casual than to say 5.9inch artillery shells This gives a feeling that the shells are nothing out of the ordinary and are very common to him.

Note (9): Brass Hats – Senior Officers. A.P.M – Assistant Provost Marshals of the Military Police.

CHAPTER FOUR

Encounters with "Piggy".

The first part of this Chapter takes Fr Francis back to his schooldays in 1890 when he was about thirteen and his first encounter with wild boar before meeting this adversary again on the fields of France.

Vividly on the present scribe's receptive mind are the distant days when the said writer was making his first acquaintance with certain word weavers of old in the class of Rudiments (10). Guest-room at Windsor, the time of return as usual cut too fine, un-willingness to disburse much potential tuck for the privilege of being jolted schoolwards in a fusty fly (11), and the promptings of a companion in like case, decided him to make a bee-line back across Her Majesty's Great Park.

We, companion and scribe, were not very sure of our topography: but things went fairly well until we found ourselves with some ten minutes to spare on the wrong side of the enclosure on Crimp Hill, wherein in those days wallowed a herd of boar.

Time pressed and none of the monsters was visible, so we got over the fence and started with what speed we might, to cross the couple of hundred yards of dangerous ground.

Half-way across, we were bogged almost to our knees, and, as we struggled forwards in the hope of finding a solid foothold, from somewhere close in front of us there rose the father of all the boars and made his un-hurried way in our direction. He moved over the churned mud twice as fast as we could, looking about the size of a well-grown rhinoceros, and we had not the smallest doubt that his intentions were unamiable.

There was a climbable oak nearby, and without unnecessary delay we were at the roomy top of the bole considering our plight, while Brother Pig nosed about the roots beneath us and masticated a shoe which my comrade had shed in the ascent. Our position had its disadvantages. We had missed Visit, and there seemed to be every probability of our places being empty during Night Studies. Our spotless jackets and flannels were a mass of ill-scented clay smeared with green lichen from the branches. I lacked a cap and my companion a shoe. In the near future there lay before us trying interviews, in which the interviewers might or might not appreciate the fact that circumstances had been beyond our control.

While, in the present, we were faced by the problem of how to evade the vigilance of our porcine guardian. Stephen Joseph (12), my companion, was plainly pessimistic. I had in my pocket a pound of particularly delectable caramels, and even of these he would have none, but as I munched I thought of many things, among them of those old Romans, whose deeds had of late been the subject of our lesson by heart in form and so at the top of my voice I invoked:

"Piggy."

'Aruns of Volsinium,
Who slew the great wild boar;
The great wild boar that had his den
Amidst the reeds of Cosa's fen,
And wasted fields, and slaughtered men,
Along Albinia's shore.'

Stephen J. besought me to stop my beastly poetry and the smitten Aruns shewed no signs of coming to our aid, but after a quarter of an hour or thereabouts there did come a keeper who recognised the school colours and having demanded our names and promised to report us, climbed over the fence, and sending the immediate cause of our troubles about his business with a sounding whack of his stick, invited us to get out.

The idea of that report passing from keeper to Ranger, and from Ranger to Rector, was distressing to contemplate. We explained the happenings which had led us to our being where he found us, begged him to be a sportsman, and tactfully as might be, proffered the twain good golden sovereigns, which by reason of our friends' visits we had between us. But to our appeals he was adamant, and our wealth he waved aside in superb refusal. However, an astute Foreign Minister has said that of all the lessons of history the story of Samson and Delilah is one of the best worth remembering for the diplomat.

As we made our way towards the gate we were met by a pretty maid, who, deciding after a brief survey that we were negligible, took our escort's hand and discoursed to him of things at large. Presently a caramel on its way from my pocket to my mouth drew her attention, and she demanded a "sweetie". Her parent was not in a position to supply her need, and I was accorded that privilege, and before we parted she had deigned to accept the whole of my store. The threatened report did not reach the Rector; our tale was received with unexpected sympathy; and we escaped with no harsher sentence than three nights at Reading Room to make up the time we had lost.

During the years that followed I may have bestowed a passing glance on the tuskers at the Zoo, or have encountered a menacing visage on the walls of some pig-sticking friend, but a quarter of a century was to roll by before I was again to come into personal contact with "piggy."

"Cambrai."

After the glorious failure of the "Cambrai Stunt" in November '17, we were moved back to a valley in the war-flattened moorland between Albert and Bray in the Somme region. Our quarters were the remains of hospital hutments, which had for some time past been

untenanted, and had been a happy scrounging ground for all the troops within a large area. Roofs had been stripped of their felt, walls were agape, windows had lost their oiled linen, or whatever material had once filled them, stoves, doors and everything movable had disappeared and the biting north wind with its load of snow penetrated everywhere.

For the first few days of our stay the only means of keeping warm lay in more or less violent exercise. Toby, of whom I have already written, was with us, likewise his pack; and a couple of weeks after our arrival he and I set out after breakfast to give them a run up the valley.

"A Run up the Valley."

We had been going for about half-an-hour, when, on gaining the top of a ridge, we saw a large black object moving away two or three hundred yards ahead. We trotted along to investigate, and as our quarry topped the rise in front Toby panted, "By Jove, it's a boar". It was five minutes before we sighted it again, and then there was no doubt that Toby was right; the pack viewed him and went away all out while we pounded along in the rear. For the best part of a mile he ran straight; then he turned and showed fight. The ground thereabouts was pitted with shallow dug-outs, relics of the fighting in 1914, many of which had fallen in, leaving cup-shaped hollows, and it was in one of these, about twelve feet across by four feet deep, that "piggy" made his stand.

When we got up, Teddy, one of the terriers, was just crawling out of the pit, gashed from shoulder to hip, the two greyhounds were dancing about wildly on the edge, doubtful of the wisdom of coming to close quarters, Tinker and Viper, yapping for all they were worth, were making dashes at their enemy's heels, and Nipper was hanging on behind, his ear flogged from side to side like a rag with a good deal of blood showing about his neck and shoulders. Toby produced a large jack knife, and jumped down to put an end to the fight, but the tusker went for him straight, and he came out more hurriedly than he had gone in.

"Toby went in with the bayonet."

For some time, the battle raged, Nipper keeping his hold, and the others giving tongue frantically with hasty attacks and retreats. It looked as if things would go on until the dogs should tire and our prey walk off at his leisure, when coming along the track we spied a labour party of Hun prisoners with their guard.

Toby sprinted over to them and persuaded the N.C.O. in charge to let him have a rifle and bayonet (13). Once more, he dropped into the arena, and again the big beast came at him, but the steel went home beneath the gleaming jaw, and after some moments of wild struggling, he pitched over kicking and squealing like a Chicago factory.

We got the pack off the noble carcase - the dogs were well content to lie and pant – and Toby stayed on guard while I went back to camp, carrying the wounded Teddy, to collect a bearer party. Rumour went around quickly that something was afoot, and half the Battalion were on the look out to greet the procession which brought the mighty beast slung on a tent-pole to "C" Company's cook-house, where the necessary rites were performed – *la curée* (14) – and the carcase hung

"To the Company cookhouse."

until it should take its place at the Company's Christmas dinner. Toby, "the spear", took the tusks, and we had liver for breakfast in mess next morning, one of the most delicately delicious things that we had ever known.

Where he had come from was a puzzle. Boar are common enough in the forests of northern France, but no one had heard of any in this area, and the most likely suggestion was that the war had disturbed him somewhere else, and that he had wandered into our neighbourhood probably along the marshes of the Somme; but he was as fat as butter, and shewed no signs of hardship or much journeying.

A week later we learnt the tragedy of our kill, when a couple of Troopers appeared in camp seeking for news of their regimental mascot, which had escaped from the waggon in which he travelled, when the Regiment had passed that way a fortnight before.

The said mascot was a huge black boar, which one of their officers had captured as a piglet during the retreat of '14. They were taken to the Sergeant-Major, whose tender heart shrank from inflicting the pain which the truth must bring. So, he assured them that no such mascot had come within our ken, gave them goodly English beer in the Sergeant's Mess and sent them happy on their bootless search; while we could only breathe a whispered prayer that when he came by his death at our hands "piggy" might not have been carrying any large amount of his Regiment's luck (15).

"The Christmas dinner."

Note (10): Rudiments was the entry class at Beaumont and a Guest-room was when the boys were allowed out to visit Windsor or possibly London.

Note (11): The fly was a light horse-drawn carriage available for hire.

Note (12): Stephen Joseph White later joined the family firm of Lloyd's underwriters. His younger brother Victor was K.I.A. with the York & Lancaster Regiment in France 1917.

Note (13): In France the traditional method of dispatching the Boar is with the *"Epieu de chasse sanglier"* a type of short sword. Rifle and bayonet seem appropriate for this situation and a *meute* (pack) of such mixed breed.

Note (14): In French venerie, this ceremony is intended to pay homage to the hunted animal and to reward the hounds.

Note (15): I can find no record as to the Regiment, though troopers indicate that it was within the Cavalry.

CHAPTER FIVE

"The animal in Man."

Fr. Francis left The M.G.C. and was attached to an un-identified Infantry Battalion for the latter stages of the War.

The rain beat in bursts on the tarpaulin that roofed our stable home, dripped through weak places, and spluttered on the oil-drum stove; the wind howled and tugged at our shelter, drove in spray-laden gusts through the shattered walls, and made our carefully shielded candles flare and gutter; and clear above the storm came the rattle of machine-gun fire and the crash and rumble of the guns.

The Medical Officer had found a brother of his craft astray and had brought him in to feed; and our guest had been discoursing to us of psycho-analysis, then something comparatively new and little known, and of the theories of its chief exponents, persons with Teuton names and minds that were typically Teutonic. The Colonel heaved himself up from his deck-chair and drained his mug before creeping off to his cellar.

"Well, Doc, it may be all very scientific and wonderful, but it seems to my unenlightened mind to be about ninety per cent wordy nonsense, and about ten per cent things we have known all our lives. I am tempted to work out a simpler theory, which I think would cover

"Well, Doc."

the facts. In my belief, we are all just the primitive savages that our remote forefathers were except that with them the cowards and weaklings went under, while with us they survive. Under a crust of civilization there lie in all who are really men, the instincts and passions of the Stone Age, and given the right stimulus they will burst through that crust like an erupting volcano".

He knocked out his pipe on the heel of an un-laced boot, and with a 'Night All,' made for the hole in the corner.

The Colonel's words may not have been strikingly original, nor yet more than partially true; but they were to receive gruesome support from events, which a few days later involved two of his hearers; and they came back to me very vividly, when three months afterwards I heard the truth about those events from an eye witness and friend.

The principal actor in them was one of our Company Commanders, whom we all knew for a very white man. Five or six years over thirty, the devoted father of a couple of bonny children, lord of the manor, magistrate, patron or director of half a dozen charitable concerns, sound sportsman, chosen friend of all the garrulous old ladies, grimy infants and stray dogs with whom we met, absolutely unselfish, devoted to the fair fame of the Regiment and the welfare of his Company.

He stood out among other splendid men; and to his other qualities he added a full six feet of lean muscle, a speckled schoolboy face of endearing ugliness, the quick resource and unfaltering pluck of the born soldier, and the shy kindness of a girl.

"A man beyond reproach."

The second player was the 'Badger,' a subaltern a few months out from public school, a tall, clean-built, good-looking boy, who was learning his trade in the Major's Company. The third, the villain of the piece, I met when the Battalion was taking part in a push of some magnitude a week after our psychological discussion.

I had been the round of my flock and had done what I could to make them ready for battle and all that battle must bring; and a few hours before "zero", being bidden not to accompany them, I had betaken myself to the advanced dressing station, where there is most chance of a priest being useful. We had had a last look round to see that all was in order; gas-curtains, tables, acetylene-lighting, the sterilizers with their glittering load of instruments, bandages and dressings, bottles and dishes, the masks for the anaesthetics, the dainty syringes with their charges of camphor oil and strychnine for cases of collapse, hot water, Bovril, blankets, biscuits, cigarettes.

"The sickly radiance of Verey lights."

All were in their places, and there was nothing left but to wait. Some threw themselves down on empty stretchers to snatch an hour's sleep, and those of us who did not feel like sleeping, refilled our pipes and talked in low voices, while the night crawled by, lit by the sickly radiance of Verey lights, and restless with the splutter of small arms and the moan and roar of an occasional shell.

The senior M.O. and I had been talking trout flies, when, looking at his watch for the twentieth time, he announced that the fireworks were due to begin. Three or four of us crawled up the low ridge which sheltered the dressing station, and hardly had we reached the top when the still night blazed into a hell of noise and fire.

As if at the touch of a finger, the level miles behind us leapt into flickering, stabbing flame, and the solid earth on which we lay seemed to rock in that shattering burst of sound; while overhead, distinct from the fury of the guns, whined and screamed and roared and rumbled shells of every size, from the vicious eighteen-pounder to the ton of metal from some naval monster far in our rear.

Then, from the high ground a mile in front of us, came an answering chorus more frenzied still, as that tempest of shrapnel and H.E. swept and plunged on front line and support, connection and shelter at ranges known to a yard.

Some few crumps came back seeking our trenches or our artillery; but for weeks we had been marking down the enemy's gun positions by aerial reconnaissance, flash and sound range. Our heavies were devoting themselves to counter-battery work to such good purpose that there were very few of his guns which the Hun could either fight or move.

When the hands of some hundreds of carefully synchronized watches should tell that thirty minutes had run out, the iron hail would lift, to plough the earth and its living load a furlong further on, and the first wave would stream over our sand-bags towards the chaotic ruin that had been a scientific system of defences.

But some of those few shells that the enemy had sent back had probably done their work, and their victims would be needing our aid, so we stumbled back to the wrecked *laiterie* where our work lay, with at least one fervent prayer that no random 5.9 would choose the same destination.

Presently cases began to trickle in, but they were consolingly few, all cheerful, and all agreed that our bombardment had smashed all attempt at real resistance, and that objective after objective was being taken at small cost.

It must have been three or four hours after day-break that a stretcher placed on one of the tables brought a gasped "My God!" from our imperturbable doctor, which made me look round at one of the ugliest sights I have ever seen. On the brown canvas in the searching glare of the acetylene, lay what had been a tall, powerfully built man. The smart grey uniform was that of a Prussian officer, the twisted hands were still faultlessly gloved, and the black and white ribbon of the Iron Cross was in its place at the edge of the tunic; but the limbs were contorted into impossible positions and the face had ceased to be a face. The man still breathed, each feeble expiration a short groan, and the blue-pencilled "M" on the bruised forehead showed that someone had injected the merciful morphia to soothe his agony.

The deft fingers of the surgeon went over it. The mouth was a shapeless gash, from which most of the teeth had been knocked out; the nose was broken; torn lids closed hollowly over the eyes and bulged out upon shattered cheeks; his shoulder was dislocated, the other arm broken at the elbow, and a thigh fractured; the collar-bone and several ribs were stove in, penetrating the lung, besides other internal injuries; and it was evident that it was a matter of hours at the most. What little could be done was done to ease his passing; and the stretcher was gently put aside till the harsh breathing had ceased and he was carried out to await burial.

A day or two later I re-joined the Battalion, which had been relieved, and was just getting into rest billets in a village half a dozen good miles behind the Front.

As I humped my pack and other portable belongings along the main street, I came across the Major, seeing, with his usual cheery care, to the housing of his men, and the boiling of a row of kettles of milk and 'buck-shee' cocoa for their refreshment. He gave me brief news of the Battalion's doings, the names of one or two who had gathered honours in the field, of half a dozen more whose harvest had been wounds, and of three who had passed beyond this life's warfare. One of these last was the "Badger", his subaltern.

That night I sat beside him at mess in a farmhouse kitchen, while the talk went around of the operations just completed, with a hundred incidents of gallantry, big tragedy, and minor comedy; and during the

"Incidents of gallantry, big tragedy and minor comedy."

months that followed I was with him constantly under very varied conditions, and he was always the same big, brave, gentle, humorous man, with never a sign of hardness in him.

Three moons passed by, and we were on a different sector, once more resting, when there came back to us a Sergeant, a particular friend of mine, who had taken a bit of iron in the shoulder when the "Badger" was killed.

From him I heard the story, which set the different pieces of the puzzle in place, and explained the nightmare condition of that Boche officer, whose injuries I had more than once discussed with the Doctor, who could only account for them as the freak result of a shell-burst. On the night of the push, our first wave had swept over the front line and support trenches according to programme with but small hindrance.

Behind the second line there was a patch of uneven ground, where the Hun, as was his custom, had constructed a maze of trenches, dug-outs, and wire, and this the lie of the land, had in great measure protected them from our fire. This obstacle lay before the platoon, with which were the Major and "Badger", and here the drama was played out.

"The Rally."

Our officers had a fair idea of the work from a careful study of air photographs; but in the grey dawn the stranger, with only a general impression of that sort of country, is at a sad disadvantage against the inhabitant, who knows every fork and turn. Trenches twisted and branched and re-joined, and there were unsuspected funk-holes, where the German lay, and hidden machine guns, against whose fire advance was impossible.

Then one of our tanks came up, floundering over trench and wire and strong point, and in her wake the platoon with bomb and bayonet got well into the position, until a stray shell scored a direct hit on the monster, blowing in her forward end and killing the crew.

It did not take the Hun long to discover that the crawling terror was out of action, and he swarmed out of holes and down communication trenches in overwhelming numbers, before which our men, their bombs exhausted, were forced to fall back.

When they rallied, in what had been the enemy's support trench, it was found that the Lieutenant was among the missing. The ground on both sides of the maze was, however, by that time in our hands; and, when reinforcements arrived with fresh supplies of bombs, and the growing light made it plain that further resistance could do no good, the discreet Teuton scuttled back or put up his hands, and the Company set to work to consolidate the captured position, while other waves surged on. Then it was that the Major, accompanied by the Sergeant and a Private, found the boy. He lay in a charred heap with half a dozen more of our wounded in the bend of a trench near the disabled tank. He was still quite conscious, though in terrible agony, but was able in broken gasps to tell what had happened.

When they had forced us out of the labyrinth, the Germans had collected our wounded on to a heap of the fine shavings which they use for bedding, had soaked the whole with petrol from the tank, and had set it on fire. This point of the story was the moment chosen by a large, swaggering Oberst to emerge from his refuge, and to advance with well-gloved hands uplifted, and ingratiating leer, and pleasant visions probably of the hospitable ease of Donington Hall (16): but when he was only a few feet away the wandering eyes of the tortured boy fell on the smirking face, and he struggled and gasped that that was the devil who had directed their torture, had jeered at them as the petrol was poured over their helpless bodies, and had kicked them back when they tried to writhe from the flames.

That, as the C.O. would have said, supplied the needed stimulus, and woke the primeval savage that slumbered beneath centuries of fine breeding in the Major's heart. He rose slowly from where he knelt beside the sufferer, and, with head forward and hands level with his chin, took a crouching leap towards the German. The latter saw his face, and the sight dispelled all hopes he may have had of a kindly reception, his hands came down to the holster at his belt, but the Major was on him like a dog on a rat. Smashing a left to his face, and seizing the hands that fumbled with the pistol, with a quick twist he forced the right arm into a hammer-lock behind its owner's back and wrenched the shoulder joint from its socket. Dropping the powerless hand, he gripped the other wrist, passed his own left forearm behind the elbow, and bearing down, snapped the bone like a stick; then stepping across he got hold of an ankle and jerked it forward with his own thigh across the front of the knee, throwing down his enemy and fracturing the leg.

What followed was bad to listen to and must have been worse to see; yet, with the reek of the burning in their nostrils, and the dying lad's moaning in their ears, it seemed so absolutely natural and just that the two onlookers felt neither horror nor revulsion, nor any instinct to arrest it. Throwing himself down on his knees upon the grey-clad criminal, the Major battered, tore and gouged with his bare hands at face and body until the features were merged in a formless shape and the cries had sunk to sobbing moans. For how long the primitive act of justice might have gone on there is no means of knowing. Actually it lasted very few minutes, for a dying sigh from the boy brought the Major back to his side, and kneeling, he held the lad's cold hands in his own, red with his murderer's blood, listened to his last faint message, and bore him the tenderest company right to the gates of death.

Less than a month ago I saw the Major on the river, punting wife, family, cocker, teddy bears, and tea basket, as happy as a child (17).

Note (16): The Hall, a fanciful Gothic style mansion at Castle Donnington, Leicestershire which was requisitioned at the start of World War 1 by the British government and turned into a prisoner of war camp.

Note (17): This would have been on the Old Windsor Reach of the Thames in 1922.

"Happy as a child."

CHAPTER SIX

"Tales and Legends."

In some earlier recollections mention was made of one James MacMorrough, Corporal in His Majesty's Royal Regiment of Artillery, and master poacher. Some indulgent readers of *The Beaumont Review* have desired further chronicles of the Corporal: wherefore these pages.

MacMorrough is far from being a typical British soldier, whose career might with profit be studied as illustrative of the ways of his kind. He is equally far from being the super-hero, whose life is worth sketching for its very superiority: he is just a very brave, very straight, and absolutely unassuming human being, into whose composition enter many virtues, a fair share of failings, and an unconscious vein of poetry. If the reader could know him well enough to penetrate the shy reserve that hedges him about and could hear him tell of the country of his boyhood, and of the happenings of his vagrant life, the writer nothing doubts that he would count the time well spent; but these things need the soft Connaught brogue, the un-studied turn of phrase, and the faith, and fire, and pathos of the teller. The excuse for these lines must be that the Editor has demanded them; and Editors as a class are not lightly to be gainsaid.

"Learning those things that are not gleaned from books."

In a little white-walled farm hidden away among the mountains that look out across the Atlantic north of Killary Bay, MacMorrough came into the world; and there for eighteen years he learnt those things that are not to be gleaned from books: the ever-changing sea, laughing, countless-dimpled, one great fluctuant sapphire in the summer noontide, moaning grey and horrible under a low roof of dirty cloud, or roaring in unearthly fury, when the western gales drove the huge breakers to meet the iron shore; the mountains that rose rampart on rampart above his home, brown, and green, and grey, and purple, as fern or heather clothed them, or their rocky shoulders stood unclad; the bogs that lay many hued in the folds of the hills; emerald valleys, where the streamlets chattered down; the mists that came billowing low from the westward, or hung in veils of mystic opal about the crest of Cruachan (18); and beast, and bird, and blossom, and the music of their voices, and the sweetness of their breath.

Nearly thirty years have passed since the lad made his way to Galway City, and there boarded the train which swept him away from all that had made up his life; but the memory of these Mayo Highlands, and their legends of saint and hero, confused at times and overlaid with the lore of other lands, is still fresh in his mind.

Much he can tell of the loves, and sorrows, and battles, and raidings of those princes and queens who lived their lives ere ever Caesar's legions tramped through Gaul. The Connaught that he knows is still the haunt of "phouka" (19). Good and evil spirits have their dwellings in its hills; and things unspeakable live, and sport, and suffer in its loughs and raths, and among the caves and rocks along its shore.

Once, in the course of its wanderings, the Battery lay for a short spell at rest, within a mile of a brook, which laughed clear above the gravel, and which should, beyond all question, have held trout.

The scribe discovered it and took MacMorrough with him to see if he could devise some scheme, by, in the absence of tackle, the hypothetical fish might be brought to the pot.

After a survey of the water, the Corporal stripped off his tunic and lay flat on the turf, his long brown fingers moving gently under the overhanging grasses and in the hollows beneath the bank. Vague memories of boyhood stirred in the writer's brain, and the two waded upstream, tickling under stones and weeds; but forty minutes' industry was unrewarded by sight or touch of a fin.

As they wended their squelching steps homewards, they discussed the basket that should have been theirs, trout they had met with, and trout in general; and then the soldier recounted how the trout came by her beauty of form and colouring:

"When Conor MacNessa was king, there came a lady to his court from the Islands of the North, and she was fairer than the fairest in the land; but she was proud and wilful and, it was whispered, more than human, sent by the powers of evil to ensnare the souls of men.

One morning, when spring was on valley and mountain, the princes were making ready for the hunt; and there before the palace in the sunlight was a great stir of the royalist of men, and of hound and horse and jewelled trappings, and horn and hunting spear, with the queenliest of women to speed them to their sport.

Then a chill came on the air, and the light lost its brightness; and looking up, men saw a rim of shadow creeping across the sun. Now there were in the King's palace wise men, who had the learning of the East, and who knew the hidden things of nature and the secrets of the stars; and, so far as memory ran, these had always foretold the passing of comets, and the falling of eclipses, and other such happenings.

The King, weak of a wound, got long years before in battle, was distressed, and sent for the sages, that they might say what this event might bode, but they could give no answer, save that according to their learning, no shadow should have darkened the sun for many long years. So, King Conor and all his court came in the gloom into the great hall; and there the written altar stone was set, and the wise ones spoke the runes and kindled the fire, as should have been done on the morrow, for on the morrow at dusk the new fire would be made on Tara's Hill (20).

"Tara's Hill."

On the altar they cast the sprigs of mistletoe and yew, and the young leaves of oak and thorn, and the other things they knew; and they read the signs of their burning, and the wreathing of the smoke. Then the oldest and wisest of them all stood forth and spoke:

'Lord King, in this hour in a land that lies beyond the sunrise, farther than the country from which our Fathers came, evil men have in their power a King, who is the master of all kings, and the ruler of all that is in earth and sea and sky.

We cannot understand this thing, for he is young and strong and beautiful, as never was king before Him, yet he has yielded Himself to them that they may work their will, and the great spirits who do Him service are withheld from staying them; and they have nailed Him to a tree thereon to die.'

Then as his speaking ceased, there broke through the wondering silence a woman's laughter, sweet as the ripple of summer waves; and the Princess from the Northland scoffed at them for dreamers of dreams, and weavers of fancies fit for the frightening of babes. And the aged seer stretched out his hand against her and foretold that for her scorning she should have no part in the fruits of the great mystery of which he spoke. So she, rising up in her silvery loveliness, went from the chamber and passing called on any there to go with her, who counted her above the old man's fond imaginings.

Now, among these nobles was a youth of the royal house, whose eyes had feasted on her beauty, and whose heart was sick with longing for her; and at her word he followed her. Then those two hastened away by the ramparts and homelands on their way towards the sea; but, as they passed through the forest, the fir trees bent down and scourged them with their branches, for the truth was known to them which the fugitives denied, since of their kin were hewn the timbers of the Cross; the briars twined about them and stabbed them with their thorns, for of their kind was plaited the diadem, which crowned their dying Lord. Straying in the darkness, bruised and bewildered, they missed the ford, and were whelmed in the river. But, in the outpouring of the Precious Blood, the waters had that day been given a new worth for the cleansing of men's souls, and for gladness would drown no living thing that came into their depths.

"The trout, their children's children."

And from that day the princess and her lover have dwelt there and shall dwell till the last men die, among the shadows of a dark pool; and the trout their children's children – and for all time they bear on their silver coats black and red marks, as their first parents still carry their wounds and bruises from briar and fir branch for their unbelief."

On another occasion, when taking a partridge from a snare, pointing to the horse-shoe mark upon its breast, the Corporal recounted how the little brown bird achieved his blazon: "Blessed St. Joseph, at the bidding of God's great angel, took the Mother and her Divine Child, and fled into Egypt from Herod's jealous wrath. All living things knew the coming of their God, and herb and tree put forth their richest flowers to deck his path, and the birds flew about Him, and heralded his passing with their songs.

Now the partridge was sad, having no song to offer; and lacking the strength of flight of the other birds, followed humbly on the ground. As the lowly cavalcade was making its way across a rocky ridge, where the road was steep and broken, the ass that bore the precious load missed its footing and was about to fall. At once the bird fluttered forward and strove with his breast to stay the slipping hooves, the ass recovered itself, and ever since, the partridge displays the print of its hoof upon his breast in memory of his service."

Many are the tales MacMorrough knows of the Saints whose lives are the fairest page in Ireland's history. The rushes, in a shell-ploughed marsh in Picardy, recalled the legend of their withered points. Over beyond in the Bog of Allen (21) once there dwelt a saintly princess, and she had an only boy, St. Monaghan, whose name lives in the land until this day. As he was at play one day beside the river, he fell, and a rushpoint pierced his eye and robbed it of its sight. His mother in her grief cursed the rushes for the evil they had done; and never since then has rush been wholly green, but always their tips are brown and sapless.

Note (18): Cruachan is the ancient capital of Connachta situated in what is now Co. Roscommon. It was named after Crochen, the handmaid of Etain, a mythical spirit maiden reborn as a mortal.

Note (19): The Irish form of a European field spirit, the kornböcke, one of various kinds of animal fairies. The phouka would appear as a goat, a pig, or, most frequently, as a horse. It would lure its victims to mount it, then take them for a wild ride and throw them off. It is possible that the word *puca* is related to Puck, another mischievous fairy figure and leprechaun, and banshee.

Note (20): Tara' s Hill in Co. Meath gets its name from Teamhair na Ri meaning sanctuary of the Kings. It is important as the traditional inauguration site of the ancient High Kings of Ireland.

Note (21): The Bog lies in the centre of Ireland between the rivers Liffey and Shannon.

CHAPTER SEVEN

"MacMorrough's Story."

In his nineteenth year there had come sickness among the stock, and the crops had done badly; so, knowing nothing of all it was to entail, young James MacMorrough had joined a party of harvesters setting out for England, where poverty and want were unknown, and where guineas were to be had for the gathering. The story of his disillusioning is an old one. The Lancashire farmers were not disinterested philanthropists, and the worth of his dreamy Connaught ways was, it seemed, higher in harsh words and jeering laughter than in the dreamt-of gold.

"Poaching a bird, rabbit or hare."

So he had parted from his companions and during the summer months had wandered from place to place, sleeping under the blue blanket, doing odd jobs that offered, and poaching a bird, rabbit or hare when he had need. Then, in the dim greyness of a September dawn near Knowsley, as he was kneeling to take a hare from one of his wires, something made him look round, and he saw a keeper within a yard of him. He was on his feet in a moment, but there was no possibility of flight, and, both unarmed, they fought as men fought before history began, punching, wrestling, kicking, without rest or rule. The fading stars died out, and soft lights, pale green and faintest rose, woke on the unseen clouds. The shadows about them took shape and colour, and there came to their unheeding ears the sleepy twittering of birds. And still they battled, the man's advantage of weight and strength made up for by the quickness and hard training of the boy. His memory of that struggle is a vague dream of blows, and pain and numbing weariness, and, over all, the ecstasy of such a combat as he had never thought these modern days could hold.

Then he recollects wakening, with soreness in every inch of him, and eyes that could scarcely see. The sun was high above him, and beside him on the trampled turf lay his antagonist. There was a pool close by, and after bathing his throbbing head, and drinking long, he turned to the grim form upon the grass. The man's face was one blood-smeared bruise, but he was breathing deep, his heart beating strongly, and his limbs were warm; yet, though he loosened his clothing and drenched him with water, the boy could not bring him to his senses. Then a great fear came upon him that the man would die, and he saw visions of the court-house and the gallows. In his panic he fled, till the sight of workers in the fields drove him back into cover. By night, he made his way to Liverpool but there he was friendless, ignorant of the streets, and afraid to ask his way to the docks, where he had some vague hope of getting on board a ship bound for Ireland or America. Everyone he met seemed to be making a mental picture of his battered features and torn clothing, while the policemen whom he passed were like the ministers of fate, awaiting her capricious rod to seize him as a murderer; so that, when a be-ribboned soldier hailed him, he fancied the dread summons had come.

"Twenty-one best years of his life."

The Sergeant's speech, however, held nothing of menace; and when that shrewd diplomat, reading trouble in his face and dishevelment, vaunted the red tunic as the surest means to cover up past sorrows, his words were as a heaven-sent message, and the lad bound himself to serve the Queen for the twenty-one best years of his life.

His way as a 'rookie' lay along no primrose path. On the square and in barracks he was the butt of the instructor and of the city arabs (22) of whom his squad was composed, until, that is, he discovered that he had natural gifts as a fighter which out-weighed the street-taught skill of his companions. Then these ceased from troubling him and the Sergeant, moved to professional interest, added science to his native equipment, and, to his own financial advantage, backed him nothing loath against novices in various Merseyside arenas.

In due course he passed off the square, and later took his place in a draft for India, and there followed years full, at least in retrospect, of incident: the sport and work and weariness, and countless happenings of Indian Army life, a little frontier war, and in their season, the lance-jack's, Corporal's, and Sergeant's stripes, with other things which he would fain have forgotten, among them a wholly unforgettable thirst.

South Africa, Egypt, Aldershot, and the depot all added to his experiences, until there came a day when he stood once more in those same Liverpool streets, with a row of ribbons on his new civilian's waistcoat, and in his pocket a few pounds, together with documents entitling him to draw a pension little more than adequate to keep him in tobacco. The Army had given him a smattering of many crafts and the mastery of none, save the one that was closed to him when he doffed his uniform, and he was at a loss as to how to seek a living.

Firstly he turned to the docks, where, it seemed, a strong pair of hands must always command a wage, only to meet with one rebuff after another. Then he encountered a former comrade, the owner of a grimy den and a "dealer's" licence, and with him he gladly entered into partnership. For a year he collected scrap metal and a limitless variety of unconsidered trifles; rejuvenated worn-out boots and tin-ware, and he fathomed the mysteries of the bone and bottle trade.

"Bone and bottle trade."

He did well in the business, and the future bade fair to see him a man of substance in a modest way; still, somehow, the long looked-for freedom failed to fulfil its promise, as compared with the ordered regularity of regimental life, while the sordidness of his slum lodging, and the unlovely jumble in the store, contrasted ill with the cleanly comfort of the Sergeants' Mess.

When the smoke of the war-torch trailed across the summer sky, and the cry for men went up from platform and hoarding, MacMorrough was among the first to answer the call. A score of years campaigning had shewn him that a gunner's lot had distinct advantage over that of his footslogging brother, besides which he feared that, if he returned to his old battalion, he might be rejected on the score of age, or be set to drill raw drafts at the depot.

So he sought out an Artillery H.Q., committed himself to a wildly inaccurate statement as to his years, and, after a satisfactory interview with the doctor, found himself happy once more in the stimulating embrace of an army shirt.

This was a time of intensive training; he already knew nearly all that was required, save the gun drill, and, almost before he could realise it, he was in the thick of war, beside which all he had known hitherto was as a picnic. The three stripes were quickly his again, but a miscalculation as to the potency of *vin blanc* resulted in his return to the rank of Gunner.

Sad to say, the same mistake, with variations, occurred on subsequent occasions; but he was of uncommon value in the handling alike of harness, horses, mules, and men; and, when the writer met him, he was a permanent Corporal, on the understanding that his lapses should be dealt with by the Padre and the Sergeant-Major, and that no word from them should reach the Orderly Room, it being understood that this weakness never overcame him except during the rare interludes when the Brigade was out at rest.

Conversation with Corporal. MacMorrough was a constant revelation of unsuspected qualities. Probably the most extraordinary of these was his quite uncanny influence over all sentient things. Once he was sent with three or four drivers to the rail-head, to take over a bunch of mules. They were big powerful beasts utterly unbroken to harness and badly demoralized by travel; and directly the R.O.D. (Railway Operating Division of The Royal Engineers)) people got them off the truck, they mixed themselves up in a squealing, kicking, biting tangle.

"Handling, horses, mules and men."

One of the rail-head staff, who tried to deal with the situation, was laid out by a flying hoof, and after that 'was none who would be foremost to lead the dire attack', which looked as if it could only result in a call for stretcher-bearers. With the unconscious carelessness of a child, the Corporal went up to the furious brutes. A pat here, a stroke there, a flow of crooning endearments, and they fell apart for all the world like a pack of well-trained forwards when the ball has left the scrum; and he took them by their head-stalls and handed them over, lathering and trembling to his helpers.

Another time, I was following up behind him when he was in charge of the limbers, which nightly rumbled back and between the ammunition dump and the gun-pits, carrying up "the goods" to feed the hungry guns. We had just passed through a village which lay on our way when there came a whizzing scream, four vivid bursts of flame in the blackness, a roar, and a cyclone of stones and mud. Three of the shells had exploded in the fallow short of the road, but the fourth had landed fairly among the leading team.

Two men were dead as they dropped from their saddles, three horses were down and the rest were plunging and struggling frantically in the traces, while the following limbers were thrown into wild confusion in the darkness. MacMorrough had reined back to see his command clear of the ruined houses, but in an instant, he had galloped up, and as if by magic the maddened animals were soon standing quiet, and the demoralized drivers had awakened to their duty, and had set about doing it. The two limp bodies were lifted out, found to be past help, and gently laid by the roadside and to my care and blessing. The two broken-legged horses were put out of their pain and, with their dead fellow, dragged clear of the track. There was no time to say farewell to faithful companions. Spare horses were brought up and harnessed in their places, a shattered wheel replaced and in a little while the ordered procession was bumping at a sharp trot clear of the unhealthy neighbourhood.

With the men it was just the same. A party, soaked and chilled to the bone in rain and mud, weary that every effort was dull agony, fed up, past caring for Officers' encouragements or Sergeants' threats, under MacMorrough's spell would straighten their aching backs, and force heart and nerve and sinew to serve their turn long after they seemed gone. Many a time, men war-sick and with nerves to breaking, have found themselves sane and confident once more after a few minutes in his company, and the hardest cases would soften to his charming.

When the unfeeling powers spoke the word that tore the writer away from his gunners, MacMorrough drove the limber that bore his kit to the railway, and that leave-taking was not the least painful of the many partings which the war has entailed. The scribe still treasures sundry brief letters, laboured over and smirched with the all-pervading mud, which shew that the Corporal has a memory for his friends.

"Bravery and kindness."

The latest, written shortly before the Armistice, records an attack of trench fever and pneumonia, and progressing convalescence in a base hospital; his discharge seems certain; and the marine-store is happily flourishing in the hands of his partner; but he doubts if he can settle down again to a life cribbed and confined by brick and mortar.

Bravery and kindness and manifold great-heartedness, it was the writer's blessing to meet among all ranks during the years he was privileged to wear the King's jacket; but he would count Corporal James MacMorrough very high in that grand company of very gallant gentlemen.

Note (22): a term used by the social reformer Lord Shaftsbury in the 19th cent. to describe "lawless slum-living freebooters ignorant of their social duties".

"The detritus of the War."

CHAPTER EIGHT

"Armistice and The Trout Stream."

"The Trout is a fish highly valued, both in this and foreign nations. He may bejustly said, as the old poet said of wine, and we English say of venison, to be a generous fish: a fish that is so like the buck, that he also has his seasons; for it is observed, that he comes in and goes out of season with the stag and buck." Izaak Walton. (The Compleat Angler.)

The glad forward rush of last November, the scribbler of these lines found himself attached to a Casualty Clearing Station, housed in the hospital of a large Belgian manufacturing town, at first things were sadly busy. All the ghastliness of wounds, gas, and sickness we were used to, and then the finish of the fighting was to bring us a new horror.

As we moved up through the country from which the Hun had just retired, we met them by ones, and twos, and twenties by the roadside; saw them singly and in bunches out across the fields, marching, staggering, crawling, west-ward over that winter landscape, gaunt, half-clad wrecks of fighting men. And directly the wards were open they poured in upon us, in their hundreds, British, French and Belgians in the main, with here and there an Italian, a Portuguese, or an ally from the East.

The German had kept them toiling with pick and shovel on trenches, and roads, and railways, dragging wagons of stores and munitions on the roads, harnessed in teams to barges on river and canal; ever driven with whip and bayonet; never sufficiently fed, without proper clothing or footgear, lacking blankets and roof by night; and at last, when the struggle was done (and he might hold them no longer), had turned them loose, hungry and foodless, in a country which he had systematically stripped bare. For the first few days most of our cases were sufferers from starvation and exhaustion. Then the influenza with its attendant pneumonia found them, and every inch of ward and corridor in the great building was packed, and doctors and sisters fought with death for those boys, most of whom were half-dead ere ever the sickness touched them.

In due course those weeks of nightmare passed. Then, as Spring brought lengthening days and fairer weather and as demobilization lessened the number of troops in the area, it became possible to look about us and to think of some form of amusement. The town itself had nothing to offer beyond numerous cinemas and a third-rate theatre, and in three directions you may go for mile after weary mile through a depressing succession of colliery villages. To the south, however, a couple of kilometres from the town the coal measures came to an end, and there are some delightful bits of grass and wood-land; *and* the stream.

"Keen fishermen."

The Commanding Officer was a keen and accomplished fisherman, and the scribbler no less keen, albeit far less skilful; kind providence put us in touch with the worthy President of the local *Société de Pêche* who have the fishing of the stream in question; and the *Société*, with much courtesy and many pretty compliments, were delighted that we as Allies, friends and sportsmen, should fish where the Boche had poached - an enemy, pot-hunter, and generally "dirty dog". So we were presented with cards of membership, overhauled the bare minimum of tackle which we had managed to carry in our kits, wrote home for what we lacked most urgently, and started out to explore.

It was an April afternoon when we first walked down the five odd miles of water, which were to prove such a Godsend to us. The trees were putting out their first touches of green, and all the country was just waking from its winter sleep. The water was big and coloured, and we saw no sign of fish or fly, except a few march browns dancing in a sheltered corner; but the whole valley was lovely then, winding deep between its steep well-wooded walls; and it has seemed almost lovelier each time we have visited it.

An electric tram took us to within half an hour's walk of the lower reaches, where the hills lie apart, and the river wanders through rich meadowlands. Here, as along much of their course, the banks are thickly fringed with alder, willow, and poplar, which make casting very difficult. For the most part, these lower lengths consist of long deep pools with sharp broken runs between them.

One of these pools in particular – we know it as the Orchard Pool – has yielded some pretty fish; to each of us a one-and-a-half pounder among others. About a mile from the bottom the stream skirts a village, above which there is a mill where iron is worked, as our fathers in the Weald worked it centuries ago, with great trip-hammers driven by water-power. The mill-dam makes no pool above it, a broad deep reach forming the needful reservoir. This stretch running at the foot of an embankment we call the Railway Pool, and here lie most of the largest, and incidentally the most un-responsive trout that we have seen. Then we come to something over a mile of water, mainly shallow and rapid where, some day when we should steel our hearts to put away the fly, we promised ourselves to do great execution with the up-stream worm.

"Cuthbert was the Colonel's particular friend."

It was here, in a smooth deep eddy at a corner, that Cuthbert had his hold. Cuthbert was the Colonel's own particular friend. He lived beneath an overhanging tangle of alder and briar. Opposite him a couple of tall willows hung halfway across the stream, and below him either bank was a veritable jungle; but Cuthbert was a noble fish where noble fish are rare. He had a noble appetite too and, whatever his brethren might be doing, he was generally to be found on the feed, dimpling the surface gently and unostentatiously, making a gourmet's leisured choice of the dainties that swept into his corner. And it came about that the Colonel on his pilgrimage was greeted by Cuthbert's slight, seductive swirl, and was beguiled into spending an hour or more hanging flies on the surrounding trees and felling the same trees as far as possible with a jack-knife. Before we left, the corner was almost fishable. Once helped by a stray breeze he did get an olive just over Cuthbert's nose, and Cuthbert took it; but, resenting the bad taste evinced in the offering of a dud delicacy to a person of his quality, he dived down among the roots, and the next time we passed that way he was absorbing neopteran with his usual staid discrimination. Cuthbert is one of the most regretted of many good friends we left behind us when our turn came to be demobbed.

Higher up we come to unbroken water running fast and deep. It should hold trout, and once the scribbler hooked and lost a good fish here; but the place is infested with diminutive roach, and you may put a blame-less fly over what you could swear to be a rising trout; but, whether the trout be there or not, one of these small pests will make a dash at it, and hook himself firmly, and, when you have dried or changed your lure, a dozen others of his kind will repeat the experiment if you give them the chance.

In a copse nearby, within a rod's length of the bank, a nightingale, fearless in the perfection of her artistry, was singing every time we passed that way throughout the summer. And then we make our way past a pumping station and lime works, both stripped of their machinery by the late benevolent occupiers of the land, under limestone cliffs with strangely contorted strata.

Pool and shallow lie beside our path but are so over-grown with bushes that there are few spots where one can get a line on the water. Then comes another mill, and half a mile or more of gently flowing water which should harbour great fish, but of which we know very little as, until late in the season, the banks were up for hay.

This is the limit of the Club water. Beyond is the demesne of a still wonderful castle, which, until the late owner tried to convert it into a Louis XVI Chateau some thirty years ago, was a perfect example of the thirteenth century stronghold.

As to what fish the river holds, we are very doubtful. For four years the Hun, true to his ideas of sportsmanship, pursued the trout with bombs, nets, and such other engines as his fancy prompted. Happily, he does not seem to have thought of lime. With one or two exceptions, who without much profit work a wet fly down stream, the members of the *Société* hardly know the artificial fly. With them *la pêche à la mouche* means two or three may-fly, grasshoppers, or daddy-long-legs fished on the bottom, generally with shot and float. Otherwise they use worm, minnow, cheese, sprouting hemp-seed and various grubs and pastes; anything in short that can be worked with rod and line.

"The river is of real chalk-stream type."

On the other hand, the river is of the real chalk-stream type, has unlimited feed, and could carry as many fish for its size as any Hampshire stream. On one or two occasions the water has seemed to be fairly a-boil with feeding fish; but it is hard to say what their size was, or how many of them were of the baser sort, though, except for the baby roach already mentioned, we landed no coarse fish. All the natives, however, speak of large barbel, bream, and chub, particularly in the lower waters.

As a rule, the trout are funny feeders, and even when the mayfly was up and for a couple of weeks it was hatching in goodly numbers, we saw very few fish really feeding — rising, that is, in the same spot or on a definite beat. More often one saw a rise and probably waited ten or fifteen minutes before the intended victim came up for another mouthful.

On the whole, fly were plentiful and varied, march brown, blue and olive dun, brown sedge, and several reddish hard-winged beetles were the most numerous, and during her short season the drake was the only subject of attention. The artificials which we found most killing were copies of the above, with the gold-ribbed hare's ear, Wickham and Greenwell (23) all rather on the larger side; small flies they seem to ignore, even on the brightest day.

The local fisherman's methods are well adapted to existing conditions, though they may seem lacking in finesse. His usual equipment is a light bamboo rod some 8ft. in length, with five or six yards of cord and gut tied to the top; a running line and reel are generally dispensed with. The rod is poked out across the stream, and the bait dropped where the angler pleases. With the same weapon, he jerks an artificial minnow about in runs and broken water. A few use the ordinary shop Devon with its bristling garniture of trebles; but the native *poisson artificial* is a deep-bellied, thin, little fellow a couple of inches long, made of pewter, with a large treble or single hook at his nose, and a hole through his tail, by which he is attached to the trace.

"Render the bait irresistible."

He does not spin, but is pulled up and down in rapid spots, and is said to be very killing in the hands of a master. Nearly everyone has his private mixture of more or less evil oils and essences, inunction by which is believed will render his bait irresistible.

Such is the stream which has given us many happy days. Not first-class fishing judged by the standard of avoirdupois – our total bag worked out at about a score of fish a piece, with an average weight of some 12 ounces; but the valley is very beautiful and is full of the wild flowers that we love at home, with big patches of daffodils in their season, and beds of wonderful small lily-of-the-valley hidden away in the copses; and there is a fair number of wild birds, dippers and kingfishers and nightingales among others. Whatever international kindnesses the war may have brought forth, we, personally, count the sportsmanship of our *Société de Pêche* as by no means the least.

Note (23): Greenwell's Glory and Wickham's Fancy Two British Wet Flies. Both of these wet flies were invented in England in the 19th Century. Greenwell's Glory in 1854 by the Rev. William Greenwell, a canon in the Anglican church. It's considered the most famous trout fly of all time, and in its dry fly version is sometimes referred to as the "British Adams." Wickhams's Fancy was invented in the 1880's by T.C. Wickham. (The "Fancy" part of the name just refers to the tinsel body, not that Wickham took a fancy to the fly.)

AFTERMATH

Fr. Francis came home from the War to find himself attached to what was known as The Mission at Farm Street in London's Mayfair for a couple of years and not far from his old family home. He then returned to Beaumont to teach at St. John's, the Preparatory school some half a mile from the main College. His friend Fr. Devas also returned together with his dog which he had smuggled with him firstly to Gallipoli and then Flanders with The Royal Inniskilling Fusiliers.

The Editor finds it of interest that both Chaplains, who took a vow of obedience at their ordination were both a little cavalier when it came to Army rules and regulations. Indeed, one General was to write of Devas, 'I don't know whether to have him court-martialled or awarded the VC'. As it was, he was not only Mentioned in Dispatches but awarded the DSO and an OBE.

The "Gen" was also safely back after four years with the Navy and Fr. Francis's brother Baldwyn was unscathed by his experiences. By coincidence, the Editor of these memoirs was to serve, many years later, in the same Regiment as Baldwyn's son.

Whether Toby came home to enjoy hunting the Shires again, we do not know, nor the future that awaited MacMorrough when he was demobbed for a second time. We can only hope that both had continued enjoyment with their country pursuits in the years allotted to them.

There is no mention in any records after the War of Fr. Francis's fishing or other sporting exploits, and it may be that any skills learnt from his Connaught friend were laid aside at that immediate time, whatever the temptation.

We do know that in his many years as a prep-school master he found a completely different interest as a radio enthusiast. Wireless was still something of a novelty between the Wars and it was written that 'from his den at the end of the gallery, he relayed gramophone and wireless music from the set he had made himself to his own class, and also had loudspeakers fitted elsewhere for the enjoyment of the boys.' It was also said that he was very adept with his hands making skilled repairs: not difficult for a man proficient at tying his own flies.

His final years were spent back at Stonyhurst: *'On a sunny summer's day on the river between the Hodder bridges, mature trees lean out from the steep southern bank, while across the wide waters an ample grassy margins shelve gently upwards. A newly-hatched mayfly flits above the fast-flowing stream whose surface breaks as a trout intercepts another. It's the perfect place for fly-fishing.'*

It would be hard to believe that Fr. Francis did not stalk those banks again accompanied by some like-minded boys or local devotee. Hunting in these areas of Lancashire was traditionally for deer, and in ages past wild boar, together with rabbits, foxes, hares, pheasants and partridges. Coverts, of a different sort from wartime France, and his erstwhile companions in those foreign fields, cannot have been far from his thoughts in his declining years.

Fr. Francis Fleming died relatively young at 64 in 1939 and was spared the Second War.

There is much written of The Great War: the courage, the misery, the failure and the success. There is also a fair record of the work of Army Chaplains and their deeds: one cannot but be moved by the exploits of the Rev. Theodore Hardy, the Orthodox Rabbi Dr Michael Adler and then Fr. Francis Gleeson who as the last officer left standing, took command of The Munsters at the First Battle of Ypres and to be forever remembered in Fortunino Matania's painting 'The Last Absolution of The Munsters' before the Battle of Aubers Ridge 1915.

"The Chaplain's Parish."

All well documented, but so little of relaxation of mind and body. The future Field Marshal Lord Wavell found it in poetry, but even he called for sport and adventure when not involved in battle. It could be said, from what he wrote, that Fr. Francis was lucky in his war, and that he spent little time in the front line, or as likely, chose not to discuss it. However, soldiers know that the time of action is short, while the waiting is long. It is of the waiting that Fr. Francis chose to write about, together with observations of some he served with, and as a country sportsman he would always have those memories, *'The years may pass and perish, but not those golden hours.'*

Another of his school contemporaries, Francis Patmore, son of the poet Coventry, wrote of the importance of these recollections at Kut in 1916 during the campaign against the Ottomans.

In England the leaves are falling from chestnut and beech and oak,
Where once 'mid mossgrown tree-trunks the ringing echoes woke,
As one brought down a rocketing pheasant, stopped a pigeon in its flight,
Or picked off a swerving woodcock as it sped into the night.

O for the smell of the mudflats when the autumn tide runs low,
As over the darkening waters the plovers come and go;
You can hear the whistling widgeon, see the teal as they cross the moon,
And that ray of liquid silver — the splash of a diving loon.

India too is calling, where the black buck graze on the plain,
Where the peacock struts 'neath the banyan and the partridge calls from the cane,
Where the jackal howls in the twilight and the flighting pintail wheel,
Where the geese fly up from the river and, circling, light on the gheel.

When the haunting smell of the wood-smoke hangs low o'er the village street,

And the dust drifts gold in the sunset, stirred by the children's feet,

When the kites swing low round the temple, and the egrets fly from the stream,

Over the silent mangoes where a myriad fireflies gleam.

These things have I known and have loved them - the heat the dust and the sweat,

The rainswept lonely marshes, the tang of dung-smoke, - and yet

If I should no more feel them, nor quaff the breeze like wine,

The memory at least is with me - for ever, for ever mine.

Fr. Francis would probably have added to that: *"Laus Deo Semper"*:
Praise be to God.

The Editor, **Robert Wilkinson**, served with the 11th Hussars and The Royal Hussars in both England and Germany before spending over twenty years living in France. He has much enjoyed country sport in all these countries. He now lives with his wife, horses and whippets on the Surrey/Sussex border. He was at school with the illustrator.

The Illustrator, **A B M P (Bertie) de Lisle**, worked as an architect in London for many years, whilst always coming back to Leicestershire. to enjoy his hunting and shooting. Now he is retired there with his wife, family, King Charles's spaniel, horses, sketching, painting watercolours and children's names and tending to his vegetable garden. His father served with the Grenadier Guards in The Great War and knew Fr. Francis.

The Editor would like to express his thanks to Bishop Richard Moth for writing the Preface, Russell Cassleton Elliott for proof reading the text and to Simon Potter MBE for his help, advice and hard work in bringing the book to publication.